Daddy, Do You Love Me?

Presented to

_____

by

_____

on

_____

In the same way, let your light shine before others, so that they may see your good works and give glory to your Father in heaven.
Matthew 5:16 CSB

Daddy, Do You Love Me?

Anita Renee Murray

Copyright © 2017 Anita Renee Murray

All rights reserved.

ISBN: 0692991573
ISBN-13: 9780692991572

DEDICATION

For Armanni - never stop believing in the greatness that lies within you. I love you.

For girls without dads - It is my prayer that you are comforted with the presence of our heavenly Father. My heart's desire is to see you thrive with love and avoid using the absence of your dad as an excuse for not reaching your full potential.

CONTENTS

Acknowledgments	8
Introduction	10
How to Use Pretty Features	13
Meet Arianna	14
Devotions	15
When you feel. . . God says	104
When you wonder daddy do you love me? Remember. . .	*107*
Reflect on God's Word Bible Scripture Reference	*108*

INDEX TO DEVOTIONS

The Wait
Nahum 1:7 JUB 15

Whisper A Prayer
2 Timothy 4:16-17a NIV 18

Breakfast Club
2 Timothy 4:16-17a NLT 22

Day by Day
Genesis 1:2-3 NLV 25

Rude Girls
Matthew 5:44 29

I'm Listening
1 Peter 5:7 NLT 33

What Color is Your Dress?
John 16:33 CEV 36

Sleepover
Ecclesiastes 8:15 NLT 40

June
Psalm 34:17 NIV 44

Excuses
Proverbs 3:5-6 NLT 48

Celebrate
Psalm 103:13 NLT 54

The Question
Psalm 34:18 NIV 60

Love is Action
1 Corinthians 13:13 BSB 64

IChat
Ecclesiastes 3:1,6 NIV 68

You Are Not Alone
2 Corinthians 1:4 CEV 72

Messed Up
Ephesians 6:1 NLT 76

Power of the Tongue
Ephesians 4:29 NIV 79

How Could You Leave Me?
Philippians 4:7 GW 83

Be Bold
Psalm 138:3 GW 86

Letters of Love
1 Corinthians 4:14 GW 90

The Point of it All
Deuteronomy 7:9 GW 98

ACKNOWLEDGMENTS

Mom and Dad, thank you so much for all of your love and support.

Wayne, my sweet husband, thank you for your love, patience and support. I love and appreciate you beyond expression.

Audrey V. Hailstock, thank you for your encouragement, inspiration, and motivation. This book would not be a reality without your unconditional love and unselfishness. Thank you for openly sharing your resources with me.

Linda Gilden and Gloria Penwell-Holtzlander, thank you for your professional writing advice.

Armanni J. Welch, thank you for being the greatest daughter in the world. Thank you for allowing me to use your experiences to encourage other girls that they can be great no matter their circumstances. Thank you for the illustrations that you have contributed to make this book beautiful.

Thank you, too, to all the readers, organizations, family, and friends who have encouraged and supported me throughout this entire process.

Most of all thank You, Heavenly Father, for putting this book in my heart and for helping me to bring it to girls everywhere. You get all the glory and honor.

"Never! Can a mother forget her nursing child? Can she feel no love for the child she has borne? But even if that were possible, I would not forget you!
—Isaiah 49:15 NLT

INTRODUCTION

I first recognized that something was bothering my daughter when we sat to have breakfast before she left for her first day of fifth grade. I fixed her breakfast and watched her zoom through the house making sure she was properly dressed and had all of her school supplies. Her smile lit up the entire house. Her good vibes bounced off the walls. I absorbed her energy to boost my morning.

As we ate, I noticed that she was no longer smiling. I sensed that something was wrong. There was a break in the silence when she whispered, "Mom where is my dad? Do you think he is thinking about me today? Do you think he cares if I have everything I need to start this school year? My heart sank as she continued to ask me questions without allowing me to answer. Mom, do you think he realizes how hard you work to give me what I need and want? What I really want to know, mom, is does my daddy love me? I fought back my tears knowing that these were valid questions of which I could not answer. This monologue led me to write this book.

Like my daughter, there are other girls who wonder where their dad is, why did he go away, is he coming back and most importantly does he love them? His absence secretly pains them. It is disheartening for these girls when they realize that their dad is alive and well but refuses to be the Dad that God called him to be. As a result, these girls are not always able to verbally express themselves, so they walk around holding in feelings that play on their emotions. These daughters wonder if they are the reason their dad left them. They may feel left out when their classmates share stories of times they spend with their dad wishing they could share similar stories. They appear happy on the outside but are silently screaming inwardly. However, no one comes to their rescue because they cannot articulate their need.

Daddy, do you love me? is a devotional for every girl who faces each day with the reality of living without her earthly dad because he abandoned her. Each devotion begins with a scripture reference which gives direction for the situation faced. A letter from God follows each experience with words of comfort and promises which encourages boldness, confidence, and strength through God's word. This will enable her to move on in the blessings of God. Love is action (1 James 3:18) and with this truth, after each letter there is an action step or memory verse designed to help girls recognize their hurt and begin to heal. Throughout the devotions, there are Bible references for reflection on God's word.

This devotional can be read all at once, one a day, or whenever faced with a specific dilemma that a child needs help dealing with. It is for those who desire a father-daughter relationship with their biological dad but feel that they are the reason he left, or their life is incomplete because their dad is absent. It speaks to those who use the absence of their dad as an excuse when things go wrong in their lives. The love that these children have for their mom is evident. They are grateful for her sacrifices. Although the lack of a dad in their life is their reality, the love of their heavenly Father comforts and encourages them to live each day in His grace.

- Anita Renee Murray

HOW TO USE PRETTY FEATURES

Pretty Features are pictured throughout this devotional. They will help you work through the experience you read about. Here are examples and descriptions on how to use these features.

Actors in television and movies are meant to entertain you. On the other hand, reality is the real-life -good and bad – situations you have first-hand experience with every day. This symbol alerts you to the reality of an event in Arianna's life.

When you smile you help change your mood from a sad one to a happy one. Being happy is showing gratefulness for the blessings you have. When you are real with yourself and you think on the goodness of your heavenly Father, you cannot help but to smile and be happy. So, puff your cheeks and show your teeth. Just smile happy.

Reference and reflect on God's promises. Each time you see this picture turn to Bible references in the back of the book for scriptures related to the promise.

Memorize scripture so that it will be easy to remember the promises of God no matter where you are.

Steps that you should take which will help you cope with the reality of your life.

MEET ARIANNA

In the pages of this book, you will read about Arianna's experiences as she copes with the voluntary absence of her earthly dad since she was in the second grade. It follows her from elementary school through her first year of high school. Through her situations she realizes that there is a word from God our heavenly Father. When she goes to God in prayer, believes His word and follows his commands, she can make it through the reality of her life without her dad.

THE WAIT

The Lord is good, a stronghold in the day of trouble; and he knows those that trust in him.
—Nahum 1:7 JUB

Arianna stood and waited for her dad to pull to the front of the afterschool pickup line as he usually did every other Friday. Today, Arianna waited longer than normal for him. When she looked around she noticed she was the only student still left waiting. "Your ride is late today, Arianna," Mrs. Rogers said. "Yes, I know. I hope my dad is alright and on his way. He promised we would go to our favorite restaurant today," Arianna replied. Mrs. Rogers walked her to the front office where she continued to wait on her dad. When her mom walked in, tears filled Arianna's eyes. She couldn't hide her disappointment. "Where's my dad?" she asked. "I don't know Arianna, I have not heard from him," her mom replied. Arianna said, "I guess he is not coming." Arianna did not understand why her dad didn't pick her up. Every day after this, he was absent from her life.

Dear Daughter,

In life sometimes, people will let you down. I know it is hard to accept. It is even more difficult when someone who is supposed to care for you hurts you. It is unfortunate your dad skipped his responsibility in picking you up from school. Don't be discouraged. I knew this day would come, and I made provision for it. I made sure your mom would be able to leave work early to pick you up. If I was not present with you during this situation and did not prepare to take care of you at this moment, you would have been waiting longer than you did. This shows you that I am always present in your life. Spending time with your dad is one of your favorite things to do, and I know you are upset. But, if you trust in me I will get you through this disappointment. Whenever you have thoughts of this day or feel that you cannot deal with the reality of your dad's absence, you can trust me. I am the source of all comfort. [1] *I will give you strength and help you through anything you face.*

Love,

Your Heavenly Father

Write It Out

On the next journal page write to your dad. Write as if you are speaking to him face to face. Tell him how you feel because he is absent from your life.

Daddy, do you love me?

JOURNAL ENTRY

Today's Date _____

WHISPER A PRAYER

And this is the confidence that we have toward him, that if we ask anything according to his will he hears us. And if we know that he hears us in whatever we ask, we know that we have the requests that we have asked of him.
—1 John 5:14-15 ESV

Arianna kneeled on the side of her bed to pray. She reflected on her stressful school day. It seemed that all her classmates talked about was the great weekend they had with their dads. Arianna could not share what she did with her dad because he abandoned her. When she finished praying she thought *does God hear me when I pray?*

Dear Daughter,

I am your heavenly Father, and I hear you whenever you pray to me. You can pray to me night or day, when you are alone or with others, when you are happy or sad. I listen with intent to protect, help, forgive, and guide you. Talk to me. Share

your problems with me. Ask me for what you need. ¹*After you pray, believe that you have received it and it will be yours.* ² *As your Father, I am open to hear any concerns of your heart even if it includes talking about your dad. Your prayer is a direct connection to me, and I will never share your requests with anyone. When you talk to me, I will talk back to you. My answers come through reading the bible, the Holy Spirit which is in you, and I may use others to share my word with you. Just whisper a prayer to me. I'm listening.*

Love,

Your Heavenly Father

Pray It Out
Say this prayer.

The Lord's Prayer

Our Father in heaven, hallowed be Your name.
Your kingdom come. Your will be done on earth, as it is in heaven.
Give us this day our daily bread.
And forgive us our debts, as we forgive our debtors.
And do not lead us into temptation but deliver us from the evil one.
For Yours is the kingdom, and the power, and the glory, forever. Amen.
Matthew 6:9-13 NKJV

Tips on How to Pray

- Acknowledge and praise God.
- Confess your sins. (God will always forgive you.)
- Thank God for all the blessings he has given you.
- Ask God for anything that you need.

Color it Out

Color in the picture on the next page. Use it as a reminder to always pray.

There is no set time to pray. You can talk to God while you are at lunch, basketball practice, or taking a walk. God is always ready to hear from you, whisper a prayer anytime.

Daddy, do you love me?

BREAKFAST CLUB

The first time I was brought before the judge, no one came with me. Everyone abandoned me. May it not be counted against them. But the Lord stood at my side and gave me strength.
—2 Timothy 4:16-17a NLT

Arianna was excited about her first day of fifth grade. Her mom ate breakfast with her in the school cafeteria. "Look, mom there is Kristen eating with her mom and dad. Mom, do you see Layla over there with her parents? Mom, there is my best friend Harmony. Can we move over there and sit with her and her parents?" "Sure, Arianna," her mom said. Suddenly Arianna stopped talking and she did not budge. "Arianna, I thought you wanted to go sit over there." She then said, "that's okay, Mom. I've changed my mind. Do you notice that everyone is having breakfast with their mom and dad?" "Well,

"MOM, EVERYONE IS HAVING BREAKFAST WITH BOTH OF THEIR PARENTS. WHERE IS MY DAD?"

they all appear to be having breakfast with both of their parents, but if you look around, you will notice that several children are eating alone," Arianna's mom pointed out. Arianna shrugged and nodded. "What's wrong? Aren't you enjoying eating breakfast with me?" "Yes, Mom. It is just that my dad isn't here with me, and all I am remembering is the day he didn't pick me up. He just left me waiting, abandoned, all alone. And I have not heard from him since."

Dear Daughter,

In the Bible when Paul, a teacher, had to defend himself in front of a judge, no one stood with him. If you picture Paul standing in a courtroom defending himself, he would appear to be standing alone. However, despite what it looks like, I was there with Paul and strengthened him throughout his trial. I know you feel abandoned and that you are missing out by not having your Dad with you like others do. But, you are never alone. I am with you and will never leave you. Take comfort in this and don't get distracted by who is not at breakfast with you. Although, you may miss your dad, enjoy this moment with your mom. Regardless of who chooses not to be part of your life, it should not take away from the excitement that you feel when good things happen to you. Some children's parents could not join them for their first day of school breakfast. You should be grateful that your mom was able to be with you. Hug your mom and thank her for having breakfast with you.

Love,

Your Heavenly Father

Write It Out

Answer the questions on the following page.

What would make you happy right now? _____

_____

_____

_____

Why aren't you happy right now? _____

_____

_____

_____

What could you do differently to be happy? _____

_____

_____

_____

Daddy, do you love me?

DAY BY DAY

> *The earth was formless and empty, and darkness covered the deep waters. And the Spirit of God was hovering over the surface of the waters. Then God said, let there be light; and there was light.*
> *—Genesis 1:2-3 NLV*

Re: "Time to wake up, Arianna," her mom shouted. "Yes, ma'am," whined Arianna, as she slowly sat up in her bed. *"Hmm, I feel weird this morning and I don't know why. Mom and I had a great time shopping yesterday and I got a new outfit."* So, *why do I feel like something is missing? she thought.* Then she realized she fell asleep with her dad's picture in her hand. "Oh, someone is missing, *him*," she grudgingly said. Arianna stuck the picture in her journal and got up to get ready for her day. She walked by the picture of her and her mom and said, "I love you, Mom, but why did my dad leave me?"

Dear Daughter,

On days like today remember me. Think back to the beginning when only I, God, existed. I then created the heavens and the earth. The earth was empty and dark. But, I spoke and said let there be light; and there was light. You are also my creation and a very special girl. It is normal for you to miss your earthly father and maybe hard for you to understand. Your dad was a very big part of your life before he decided to leave. You enjoyed his cooking your breakfast in the morning and dinner at night. You should always keep those memories of happy times and use them to help you get through your feelings of emptiness. Your mom is there to cook for you and to love you, and she does that joyfully. I spoke light in the world and I speak life into you. Fill yourself with my presence for I will never leave you nor forsake you. I am right here with you even now. [1]

Love,
Your Heavenly Father

Remember God can take your emptiness and fill it with joy. Just call His name and trust in Him.

Think It Out

1. What if there was only one color in the world. Everyone wore the same color. Food was all the same color. Your toys were the same color. The traffic light would never change because only one color existed. We would only have night because there would be no light. On the lines below describe how this world would look.

_____
_____
_____

Now, think about all the colors that we have. Look at all the different colors of your clothes. Look around your house how many different colors are there? We have day and night because there is light.

2. Look at the two pictures on the next page. Title one "Before God Spoke" and the other "After God Spoke." Why did you choose to title the pictures the way that you did? Which picture do you like better?

_____
_____
_____

3. What does this exercise teach you about the things that happen in your life?

_____
_____
_____

Title: _____

Title: _____

RUDE GIRLS

But I say unto you, love your enemies, bless them that curse you, do good to them that hate you and pray for them which despitefully use you and persecute you.
—Matthew 5:44

Arianna ran in the house, straight to her room and slammed the door. Her mom opened her door and asked what was wrong? Arianna sobbingly replied, "They keep picking on me. The other girls on the bus called me ugly and said that's why my daddy left me."

Dear Daughter,

You are my creation and you are beautiful in my sight. I know people can be mean sometimes. Unfortunately, some people look for ways to bring others down. They have no reason to hate you but do because they are unhappy in their own lives or your happiness makes them upset. [1] *No matter the reason someone mistreats you, don't let it keep you down. I know it may not feel nice when others hurt your feelings, but some people disobey my commandments and are rude. I command my children to love*

their neighbors as themselves. ² *Loving your neighbor means treating others as you want to be treated. As you grow older, you will see that not only are girls rude, but boys can be just as mean. The truth is words can hurt.* ³ *When you are picked on, or mistreated don't become angry. You cannot control what others say or the fact that your dad left. You are not the reason for his absence. He made that decision on his own. You can only control your words and how you react to someone else.* ⁴ *Continue to pray for him and those who are rude to you and be nice toward others despite their response. Love your enemies and those who mistreat you. If you find difficulty doing this, pray to me for help. I will guide you.*
Love,
Your Heavenly Father

When someone is being rude to me, I will recite this verse and know that God has it all under control. You should too.

Matthew 5:44
But I say unto you, love your enemies, bless them that curse you, do good to them that hate you and pray for them which despitefully use you and persecute you.

Daddy, do you love me?

Write It Out

Complete the "I Am Poem" by filling in the blanks with positive words about you. The last four have been filled in with promises from your heavenly Father.

I AM POEM

I am_____.

I am a child of_____.

I am a friend of_____.

I am_____.

I think_____.

I feel_____.

I care_____.

I am_____.

I am_____.

I am <u>chosen</u>. I am <u>wonderfully made</u>.

I am <u>beautiful</u>. I am <u>destined for greatness</u>.

I am <u>all that God said I am</u>.

Arianna's Example "I Am Poem"

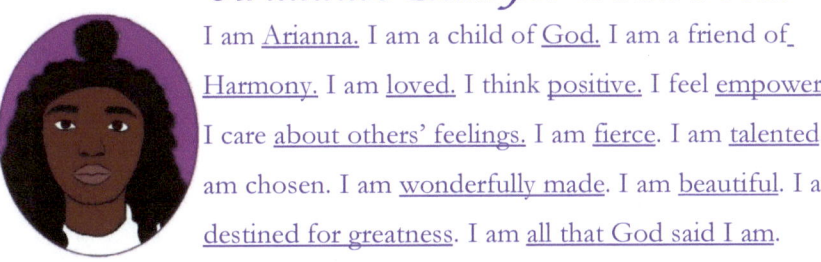

I am <u>Arianna.</u> I am a child of <u>God.</u> I am a friend of <u>Harmony.</u> I am <u>loved.</u> I think <u>positive.</u> I feel <u>empowered</u>. I care <u>about others' feelings.</u> I am <u>fierce.</u> I am <u>talented.</u> I am chosen. I am <u>wonderfully made</u>. I am <u>beautiful</u>. I am <u>destined for greatness</u>. I am <u>all that God said I am</u>.

Talk It Out

Look in the mirror and repeat this:

I am beautiful.

I am wanted.

I am loved.

I am not responsible for anyone who chooses to leave my life.

I can only control my actions.

I am destined for greatness and I am all that God said I am.

Write these sentences on an index card and put it where you can see it every day.

Treat others like you want to be treated. Regardless of how they treat you.

I'M LISTENING

Give all your worries and cares to God, for he cares about you.
—1 Peter 5:7 NLT

R: *"Hello. Hello.* Arianna are you with us?" her mom asked. Arianna jumped, "Yes, Mom, I'm here." You are deep in thought over there. What are you thinking about? "Nothing," Arianna mumbled. "Is there something wrong with you?" her mom asked. Arianna shrugged her shoulders and said, "No." Arianna's mom could tell something was bothering her, but Arianna would not share. Arianna really missed her dad but did not know how to share it with her mom.

Dear Daughter,

One of the most important relationships you will have is with me. When you feel that your mom just does not understand. When you feel that you are all alone and have no one to talk to, remember I am here. I care. I am listening, talk to me.

Love,

Your Heavenly Father

Pray It Out

Dear God, my Heavenly Father. Thank you for caring for me.
Today, I really missed my dad, and although my mom is here, I felt all alone. I am glad to know that I am not alone and that you are always listening to me. I need you right now. Comfort me and fill me with your love. Amen.

Write It Out

On the next page write out how you are feeling and what has made you upset.

Daddy, do you love me?

Right now, I am feeling: _____

_____

_____

_____

_____

_____

I feel this way because: _____

_____

_____

_____

_____

What can you do now to smile happy? _____

_____

_____

_____

_____

WHAT COLOR IS YOUR DRESS?

I have told you this, so that you might have peace in your hearts because of me. While you are in the world, you will have to suffer. But cheer up! I have defeated the world.
—John 16:33 CEV

Today is the big day, the big dance. All week Arianna's friends have been talking about the Father-Daughter Dance that takes place tonight. She was perfectly fine when they talked about it during lunch and in-between classes on the previous days. She brushed it off because she knew that she would not be going. But today was different. It seemed that during recess everyone came up and asked "Arianna, what color is your dress?" Then it finally hit her that she will not be going to the dance with her dad. Arianna thought, *I didn't go to the store with my dad to pick out a pretty dress in my favorite color. And I didn't make-up a cool dance routine with him.* Tears streamed down her face and she softly replied to her friend that she would not be attending because her *dad* cannot make it. Fed up with all the questions about her dress, Arianna walked away wishing the school day would hurry up and end.

Dear Daughter,

I know tonight there is a special dance at your school for fathers and daughters. It should have been a day on which you wear your favorite color dress and dance with your dad. But, because your dad won't be there, you have had a very sad day and you don't want to be bothered by anyone. It is difficult to talk to others about your dad's absence. I know all about your frustration, and I have not left you. Cheer up. I have overcome the world. There is nothing that you face that I cannot handle. Although, you may not be able to go to this dance with your dad I will give you other opportunities to dance with those you love. There are family events, birthday celebrations, graduation and many other places where music will play, and you can have your dance with your grandfather, uncle, cousin, best friend or whoever you want. It will be your choice and you will have on your favorite color dress and it will be an enjoyable occasion. Have joy in me for I am your strength. [1]

Love,
Your Heavenly Father

Dance It Out

Look in the mirror. Give yourself a big hug. Rejoice. Take a swirl around the room. Go give your mom a big hug and tell her you love her. Then put on your favorite song and ask your mom to dance with you.

Snap It Out

Take a selfie of your beautiful smile. Save it as a wallpaper on your phone. When you are feeling sad, look at your picture and think on how much you are loved. If you cannot take a selfie draw a self-portrait and tape it to your mirror as a constant reminder of the love that surrounds you.

Pray It Out

God thank You for a brand new day. Thank You for a mom that loves and cares for me. Lord, help me to remember that no matter how frustrated I may feel about the absence of my dad, You have all power. And in You, I can have peace. Amen.

A delay does not mean a denial. Things may not occur when you want them to, but God's timing is perfect.

SLEEPOVER

So, I recommend having fun, because there is nothing better for people in this world than to eat, drink, and enjoy life. That way they will experience some happiness along with all the hard work God gives them under the sun.
—*Ecclesiastes 8:15 NLT*

Arianna spent the night at her best friend's house. This was the first time her mom allowed her to go to a sleepover. Arianna had a big smile on her face as her mom pulled into Harmony's driveway. She jumped out of the car, ran and rang the doorbell. Harmony greeted Arianna and they went into her room. They were having so much fun. "It's time to cook," called Harmony's dad. They helped cook and set the table. Arianna ate quietly. Afterwards, all three of them sat and watched a movie. Harmony noticed that Arianna was not talking, and she looked unhappy. She jokingly asked, "Are you homesick, Arianna?" Arianna replied, "No, I am fine." They continued to watch the movie and went to sleep. The next morning Arianna's mom arrived to pick her up.

Daddy, do you love me?

Dear Daughter,

Sometimes things or people may remind you that your dad is not a part of your life. But don't let that get you down. No matter how you may feel because you cannot do special things with your dad anymore, like cooking and watching movies, you should not let that keep you from having a good time with the ones you are with. When someone you know shows you good intentions, kindness and wants to include you, embrace it. Don't waste time being unhappy about who does not want to be in your life. Enjoy every moment when you are doing things that you love with the ones you love. I will put the right people in your path who will help you laugh, have fun and who you enjoy being around. Trust in me and have fun in the life that I have blessed you with.

Love,

Your Heavenly Father

Proverbs 3:13 HCSB

Happy is a man who finds wisdom and who acquires understanding.

Read It Out

A Poem for You

BE HAPPY

When you are happy, show it

When you are having a good time live it

When you begin to think about what you don't have, forget it

When you wish your dad was present, pray about it

When you miss hanging with your dad, remember the good times

When you want to talk to your dad, call on God

God will give you peace, God will comfort you, and God will mend

your broken heart

Once you have done all of these things find you mom.

Hug her, kiss her and tell her you care

Tell her you are glad that she is always there

Daddy, do you love me?

Write It Out

On the curved lines below write in 6 things that makes you happy. Use the smiley face to remind you to smile happy.

JUNE

The righteous cry out, and the Lord hears them; he delivers them from all their troubles.
—Psalm 34:17 NIV

R: Arianna turned the calendar to the new month and sighed, "June, another Father's Day without my dad." Arianna continued speaking softly to herself. "June is such a hard month for me. I mean I love my granddad and my uncles. I enjoy making cards for them each year. But, it's just not fair. My dad is alive and well but just disappeared from my life." Arianna drifted away in a daydream. Images of talking to her dad on Father's Day surfaced. She mentally asked her dad:

I wonder how he would respond to my questions.

Daddy, do you love me?

Arianna pondered these questions because they are too hard for her mom to answer. Drifting back to reality Arianna whispered, "I want to hear his voice, see his face, and embrace him with a hug." Arianna laid in bed and drifted away again.

> Dad, I wish you could hear me now, celebrating Father's Day is an honor. I want to share it with you. I want to shower you with gifts on this day and love throughout the year. But instead, I have to listen to my friends share the wonderful things that they are doing for their dad's. This makes me sad. When others ask me what I have for you, I begin to cry because I have no reply.

> As I sit silently, I think on all the good things that my mother does for me. My mom is awesome, but I miss you, Dad. After all, I am the reason you should be allowed to celebrate this day, but you are not allowed to because you are just a deadbeat dad. And there is no such thing as deadbeat dad's day. Deadbeat dads don't deserve the right to celebrate because they cause emptiness and pain.

> I did not tell you to go away. That was a choice that you made. I am your daughter. You and mom created me. Mom is the only one who cares for me. She can look in my eyes and see love and forgiveness that is clouded by disappointment and unanswered questions. Do you realize how much you are hurting me? Do you even care? Daddy, do you love me?

You can always talk to your mom about your feelings for your dad. She will not get angry or upset.

Love Notes

Dear Daughter,

I hear your cry. I know you hurt and feel the void of not having your dad. I did not make a mistake when I chose him to help create you. I gave him the responsibility to raise you, love you and be there for you every day not just on Father's Day. He chose to ignore my command and go his own way. I am near to you for every heart ache or celebration. Do not be discouraged. Above all, I'm your heavenly Father and you are my child. ⚷ [1] *I will help you through this month and every day of your life. Continue to show love to the father figures – mentors, uncles, and grandparents I have placed in your life. As you do this you honor them, and you glorify me.*

Love,
Your Heavenly Father

Write It Out

In the journal entry space provided write to your dad as if you were speaking to him face to face. Tell him exactly how you feel about you not celebrating Father's Day with him.

Daddy, do you love me?

JOURNAL ENTRY

Today's Date _____

EXCUSES

Trust in the Lord with all your heart; do not depend on your own understanding. Seek his will in all you do, and he will show you which path to take.
—*Proverbs 3:5-6 NLT*

"Arianna, please stop tapping your pencil on the desk," Mrs. Wars sternly said. Arianna grunted. The bell rang. Arianna barely made it to her next class before the tardy bell. "Arianna, you should be seated and ready to start class before the last bell rings," Mr. San warned. "Ok," she sharply replied. Arianna was inattentive and doodled the entire class period. When she made it to her final class of the day, she was called out by her teacher for not completing her assignment.

The next school day was a repeat of the day before. During lunch Arianna asked if she could go to the guidance counselor's office. Arianna shared with the counselor that she was missing her dad and had been thinking a lot about him all week. She said his absence is the reason that she cannot focus in class. Arianna's mom was called and advised of Arianna's behavior and visit with the guidance counselor.

Arianna and her mom had a conversation about what was

happening at school. Her mom said, "You have always been an excellent student, and sixth grade should be no exception." She reminded her of all her accomplishments and told her that she cannot use the absence of her dad as an excuse for receiving low scores on assignments and not participating in class.

Dear Daughter,

I am aware that you miss your dad and you still want him to be active in Your life. [1] *It is perfectly normal to have these feelings. You had great times with your dad. It is difficult to deal with the reality of someone who suddenly disappears after being a constant presence in your life. Your dad's voluntary absence did not catch me by surprise.* [2] *I knew you would experience feelings of abandonment, and I am still here with you. I will comfort you and heal your wounds. In the midst of your feelings, you must not allow circumstances or people to deter you from the plan I have for your life. Don't blame the absence of your dad for things that you can control. Keep your mind on positive things and work hard.* [3] *Don't concern yourself with things you cannot control or things that only I, your heavenly Father, have power over. Even when things don't feel good it is still working for your good.* [4] *This means that I am working everything out on your behalf to give you hope and a future. Depend,*

believe, have faith in me and you can do all things that I have destined you to do. ⁵ *When you fall off track or become distracted by things that you cannot control, whisper a prayer to me. Ask me to help you, and I will direct your paths.*
Love,
Your Heavenly Father

Excuses does not release you from the responsibility of an assigned task. Work hard at whatever you do. Seek help when needed. Never settle for less than God's best for your life.

Write It Out

There are two target boards pictured on the following pages. In the first target board, write 6 positive things in your life right now. In the second target board write in 6 things that you want to accomplish within the next year. Under each picture write at least 3 things you need to do to have positive vibes and to focus on your goals. When you are feeling down or distracted use these images as reminders that
(1) only you can control your thoughts (2) everything is working for your good and (3) God has great plans for your life.

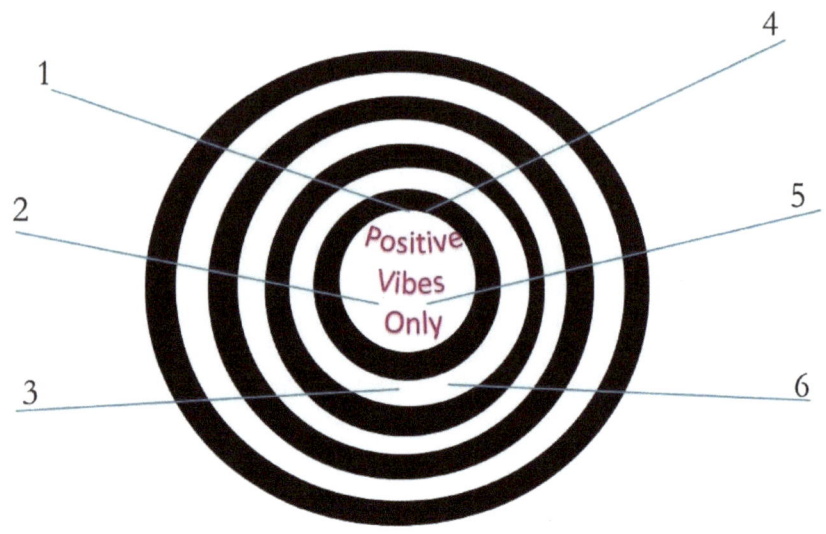

1. _____
   _____
2. _____
   _____
3. _____
   _____

Daddy, do you love me?

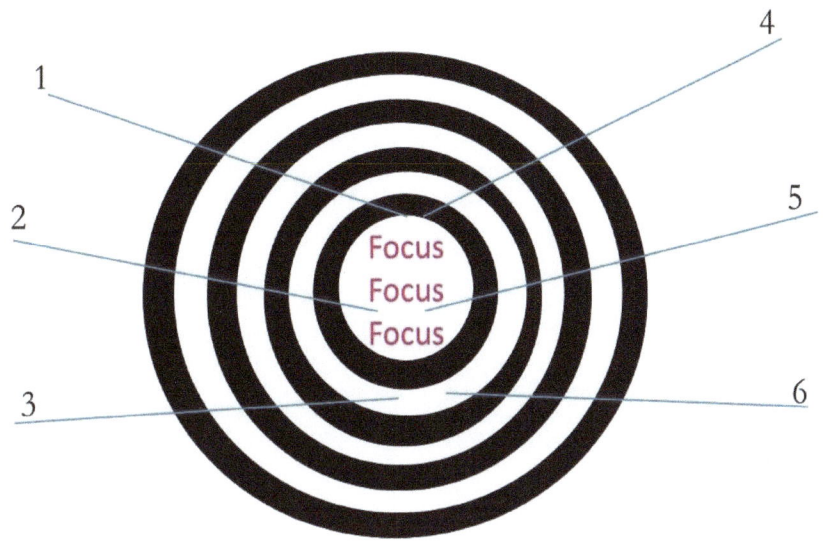

1. _____

_____

2. _____

_____

3. _____

_____

God has equipped you for everything you are going to face. You have the victory.

Love Notes

CELEBRATE

> *The Lord is like a father to his children, tender and compassionate to those who fear him.*
> *—Psalm 103:13 NLT*

Re: *Hmmm, there is something special about today, but I cannot remember what it is?* Arianna thought. "Mom, what is so special about today's date?" she shouted. "I don't know Arianna, look at your calendar. Maybe you wrote it down," her mom replied. Arianna turned the pages in her planner. Scribbled in the Notes she read dad's birthday. She slumped down in her chair. "Wow, I would love to say happy birthday to him. Too bad he left me. But, I would really like to celebrate with him. 'Reality check," Arianna said as she looked in the mirror. "He doesn't want you to be a part of his life," she pouted. She shrugged her shoulders, forced a smile and got ready for school.

Daddy, do you love me?

Dear Daughter,

It is nice of you to remember your dad on his birthday. I also understand why you are disappointed. There is nothing wrong with missing your dad and desiring to celebrate with him. It is natural for you to want to share his birthday with him. Birthdays are times to celebrate. Your dad is missing out on the blessings of having you as a daughter by staying away. Fortunately, you have some good memories that you can reflect on. My daughter, I am compassionate towards you, and I understand that you are longing for love from your earthly dad. In his absence, lean on me for I am humble and gentle at heart. You will find love and healing in me. ¹ *Share with me your good father-daughter memories. Sing a birthday song in honor of him. Don't hold a grudge toward the absence of your dad. Celebrate, forgive, and continue in love.* ² *I have blessed you to see this day. Rejoice and be glad.*

Love,
Your Heavenly Father

Whisper A Prayer

Dear God, thank you for creating my dad. If it wasn't for your creation, I would not exist. I pray that my dad is having a happy birthday. God, I pray that he will seek you regarding his absence from my life. God, if it is your will, I pray that you work on his heart and give him the desire to have a healthy relationship with me. Most of all, God, help me to love my dad, forgive him and not to harbor any hate towards him. Amen.

It's okay to cry. Crying is a form of healing.

Daddy, do you love me?

Color It Out

Color the birthday card. In the empty space write him a message. Tell your dad how much you miss him and love him. When you want to celebrate look at it and add to it each year on his birthday.

Trouble don't last always. Tears may flow in the night, but joy comes in the morning. Celebrate in the Lord. He is working everything out for your good.

Wishing you a happy birthday Dad... wherever you are.

Continue the birthday message in your own words.

THE QUESTION

The Lord is close to the brokenhearted and saves those who are crushed in spirit.
—Psalm 34:18 NIV

R: Arianna was excited. She was invited to paint eggs with some other children. After they painted the eggs they had an Easter egg hunt. Arianna love painting eggs, but she love searching for them even more.

As Arianna and the other children carefully painted the eggs, they chatted. Then one of the children asked her, "Arianna, where is your Daddy at?" Arianna burst into tears and ran into the bedroom. Her mom immediately followed her. Although this experience was equally hard for her mom, she comforted Arianna.

Dear Daughter,

I saw how excited you were about painting and hunting Easter eggs today. I also knew that someone would ask a question about your dad. ¹I know it breaks your heart every time someone asks about him and you cannot answer. ²Many people including children notice that you and your mom are always together. You both go to church, out to dinner, to the movies, and to other events. Your mom is always at your games and performances. It is a blessing to have your mom support you in everything that you do. Some children have a mom and dad in their home, but like you, some children only live with one parent. This could be for different reasons. When people notice things are different than what they think is normal, they ask questions. Now, adults may be a little more thoughtful when asking these questions. But, children are to the point and sometimes can be a little harsh. These children do not mean to hurt anyone, and they are not trying to hurt you when they ask you this question. At their age, they are not able to carefully choose their words when asking questions. You should forgive them and not take offense to their inquiry. Daughter, you are not feeling this pain alone. Your mom's heart also breaks every time you are confronted with this question. She wants to come to your defense, but it is difficult for her to do. Instead, she reaches out to comfort you, just as I do. When feelings of hurt resurface when you are asked the question, remember I am near. When you wish, the questions would stop, be strong. Don't let it distract you. Take comfort in knowing that I will heal your broken heart. Enjoy the moment that you are in. I am with you always even when your spirits are down. Whisper a prayer to me. Love,

Your Heavenly Father

Fill in your response to the questions.

THE QUESTION

Where is your dad? will be asked. It may be asked by adults, children, friends, or family. The key to coping with the pain associated with this question is to face it. The questions in the text conversation are intentional, although you may not know the answer. Write your response to each text message that you are able to answer. If you do not know the answer simply write IDK (I don't know.) But, attempting to answer these questions will help you in responding to the question when you are asked.

Daddy, do you love me?

Transcript

Person: Where is you dad?

You: _____

_____

You could say: I don't know where he is at today.

Person: Why did he go away?

You: _____

_____

You could say: He left because he wanted to.

Person: When are you going to see him again?

You: _____

_____

You could say: I have given all of that to God to handle.

The more you face these questions on your own, the less you will be caught off guard when someone asks you these questions.

LOVE IS ACTION

And now these three remain: faith, hope and love; But the greatest of these is love.
—I Corinthians 13:13 BSB

R: During her last class period, Arianna received her invitations to the eighth-grade graduation ceremony for her family members. She also received a letter listing all her accomplishments along with the awards she would receive at the ceremony. "Yes, I made it eighth grade graduation. I can officially say good-bye to middle school. And I am getting certificates, metals and a trophy." Arianna met her mom at the door and showed her the invitations while waving her letter of accomplishments in the air. Then suddenly she stood still, and her mood changed. "What is it?" her mom asked. "I wish my *dad* could see me now. Mom, why doesn't my dad love me?"

Dear Daughter,
I understand that during this time of celebration of your hard work you are missing your dad. I know that you wish to share this accomplishment

with him, and his absence makes you angry. You may never understand the reason he left or why he doesn't show love toward you. My child, this should not be your concern. Don't allow these times to dampen your spirit. Appreciate and be grateful for those who choose to be in your life. Always remember, no matter what, you are loved. Love is shown through actions. [1] You know this is true because your family showed up to support you in your moments of success and are there when you need them. Rejoice in these facts. Celebrate your hard work with them. Accept your awards with joy. I have placed the right people in your life at the right time. Remember, even in the absence of your earthly dad, I am your heavenly father. I am with you always and will love you, provide for you, and protect you all the days of your life.

Love,

Your Heavenly Father

Accomplishing a goal big or small is reason to celebrate and have a good time.

Read It Out

A Poem for You

CHERISHED DAUGHTER

My dearest daughter

I cherish you so

I know that some days you may be sad,

you may want your dad to call,

Some days you may want your dad to spend time with you

This is normal, and you should not feel bad about these desires.

Cherished daughter on these days remember you are precious in God's

sight and you are his delight

Your earthly dad maybe absent, but God is always present

Rejoice in this fact and share in God's love that surrounds you

Color It Out

ICHAT

There is a time for everything, and a season for every activity under the heavens: a time to search and a time to give up, a time to keep and a time to throw away.
—Ecclesiastes 3:1, 6 NIV

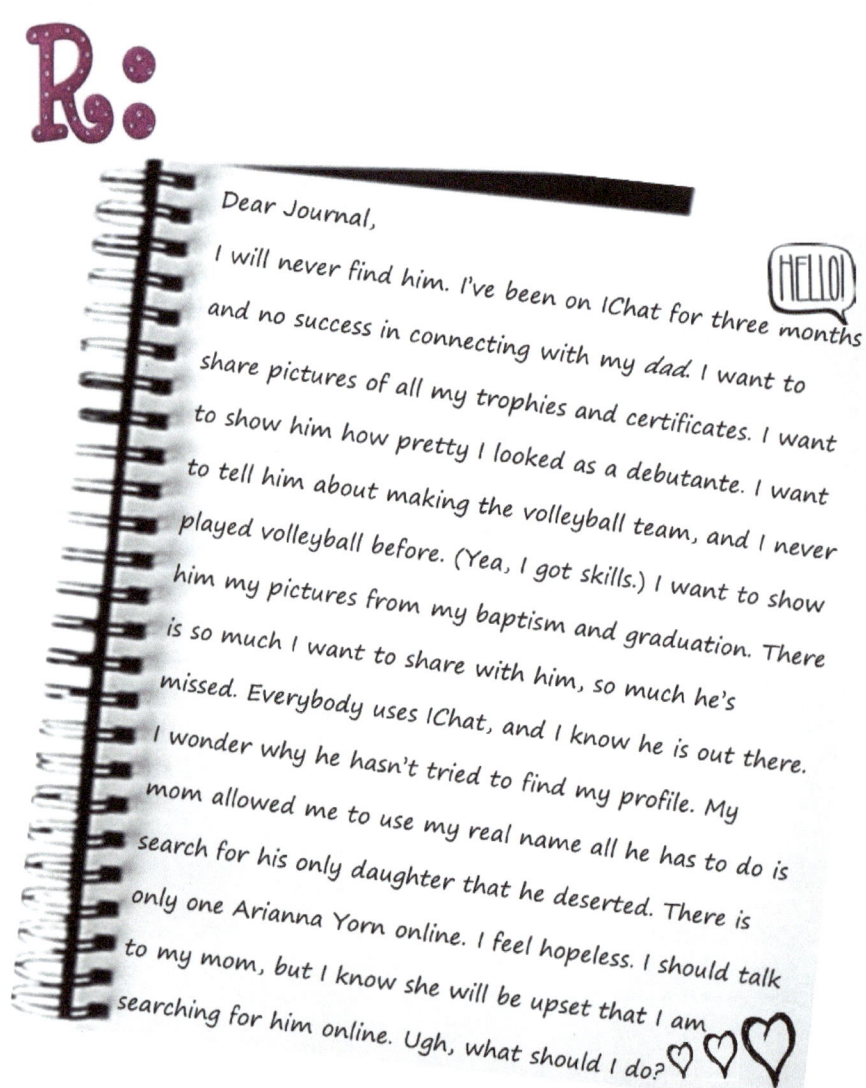

Dear Journal,

I will never find him. I've been on IChat for three months and no success in connecting with my dad. I want to share pictures of all my trophies and certificates. I want to show him how pretty I looked as a debutante. I want to tell him about making the volleyball team, and I never played volleyball before. (Yea, I got skills.) I want to show him my pictures from my baptism and graduation. There is so much I want to share with him, so much he's missed. Everybody uses IChat, and I know he is out there. I wonder why he hasn't tried to find my profile. My mom allowed me to use my real name all he has to do is search for his only daughter that he deserted. There is only one Arianna Yorn online. I feel hopeless. I should talk to my mom, but I know she will be upset that I am searching for him online. Ugh, what should I do?

Daddy, do you love me?

Dear Daughter,

I know you are excited that your mom finally allowed you to get an iChat account. You should enjoy this freedom responsibly so that you do not lose your privileges. I also know you are anxiously hoping to connect with your dad. You would probably be happy if you did. Be careful, connecting with people on social networking sites can be risky. There are dangerous people online who could be plotting to harm you. ✑ [1] This could also be a painful wait time, and it may never happen. If I had destined you to connect with your dad on social networking within the last three months, it would have happened. Although you think you are ready, I know that you really aren't, and your dad isn't either. Continue to strengthen your relationship with me through prayer and studying my word. Pray for your dad that he strengthens his relationship with me and seek me for restoring his relationship with you and be the Dad that I called him to be. Don't concern yourself with things you cannot control, but rather focus on what you can. Enjoy life and the moments you spend doing things you like to do. Try not to make everything you do a chance to look for your dad. My thoughts are completely different from yours and my ways are far beyond anything you could imagine. ✑ [2] There is a right time for everything. I know what is best for you, and I have your best interest at heart.

Love, Your Heavenly Father

Talk It Out

Talk to your mom. Tell her that you were searching for your Dad online. Your mom may be upset with you, but she would appreciate you for telling her. This will open up conversation to discuss your dad and you can express feelings that you may have been holding in. In addition, your mom will be aware what you are doing, and she can help keep you safe online. After talking to your mom, answer the questions on the next page.

You should never share personal information or pictures online with someone you don't know and trust.

Write It Out

Q: Why is it dangerous to meet in-person with someone you found on the internet?

A:

A:

Q: Should you share your personal information such as phone number and address with someone you do not know in person? Why or why not?

Anita Renee Murray

YOU ARE NOT ALONE

He comforts us when we are in trouble, so that we can share this same comfort with others in trouble.
—2 Corinthians 1:4 CEV

R: Arianna was excited about her first day of high school. She met a new student and they quickly became friends. They both were in the band and played basketball. Whenever they were together they talked about music and sports. Arianna was glad to meet someone who she had a lot in common with. Listening to music together one-day Michael Jackson sang:

"How could this be? You're not here with me. You never said goodbye. Someone tell me why; did you have to go? And leave my world so cold."

Arianna stopped dancing and sat on the chair. Journee asked, "Are you tired already? We just started." Arianna replied, "No, I'm not tired. It's just every time I hear this song, it reminds me of my dad. He went away." Journee whispered, "My dad went away too. He was supposed to pick me up from school, and he never came. That happened five years ago." Arianna said, "Wow that is the exact same thing that happened to me seven years ago."

Dear Daughter,

It is not a coincidence that you and Journee met and have so much in common. I created people in my image so that you do not have to go through anything alone. [1] *You are not the only one who has to deal with the absence of your dad due to his selfishness. I know everything about you including the number of hairs on your head.* [2] *I sensed that you both needed someone in your life who could relate your reality of being a high school student without your dads. This is me showing you my love in action. I will always provide for you whenever you lack.* [3] *I will surround you with positive influences and peers that can relate to you and who you can relate to. Talk to me when you are going through unexplainable emotions. Continue to pray for anything you need or go through. I will never leave you or abandoned you.*

Love,

Your Heavenly Father

Remember God can take your emptiness and fill it with joy. Just call His name and trust in Him.

Psalm 23 GW

The Lord is my shepherd. I am never in need. He makes me lie down in green pastures. He leads me beside peaceful waters. He renews my soul. He guides me along the paths of righteousness for the sake of his name. Even though I walk through the dark valley of death because you are with me, I fear no harm. Your rod and your staff give me courage. You prepare a banquet for me while my enemies watch. You anoint my head with oil. My cup overflows. Certainly, goodness and mercy will stay close to me all the days of my life, and I will remain in the Lord's house for days without end.

SEARCH IT OUT

Complete the Word Search puzzle -with words from Psalm 23- on the next page.

Daddy, do you love me?

PSALM 23 GW

```
S B A S O B J D J C R E M A N
P S A N E E R A O S E E G I E
X K E S O E R U E W M O M M Q
E S I N H I R E S E A G A N X
G D J P S A N E U N I O C S Q
E L E O G U M T O E N O E S Z
E H H E S H O H H R V D Q W E
S Y H D S P Z E S M I N N O I
P A S T U R E S T U P E E L Y
V A L L E Y E A G H Y S E F U
B G N E E R G T C Y G S D R L
S O U L D M L T A E C I E E T
I T J R P R K I U W F R R V T
J A O C Q Q C Q F V U U E O Q
H L T E U Q N A B E G N L M Q
```

WORD BANK

ANOINT	BANQUET	BESIDE	COURAGE
GOODNESS	GREEN	GUIDES	HOUSE
LIFE	LORD	MERCY	NAME
NEED	OVERFLOWS	PASTURES	PEACEFUL
REMAIN	RENEWS	RIGHTEOUSNESS	
SAKE	SHEPHERD	SOUL	VALLEY
WATERS			

MESSED UP

Children, obey your parents because you belong to the Lord, for this is the right thing to do.
– Ephesians 6:1 NLT

Re: Arianna, come here! Arianna knew she was in trouble, but she was not sure what she did wrong. Arianna walked into her room and saw her mom sitting at her desk staring at her computer and shaking her head. The messages that Arianna and Reggie were sending each other showed on the screen. Arianna dropped her head and reluctantly said, "Yes, mam?"

Dear Daughter,

In the bible, my son Abram is a good example of the benefits of obedience. When Abram was 75 years old, I told him to move from the home he had known his entire life. He had to leave behind material possessions, family and friends. If he did this I promised I would make him famous and that he would be a blessing to others. Abram did what I told him to do and I kept my promises to him.🎵 ¹ In life, you will have to do things that you do not want to do. Regardless of friends you have who try to convince you otherwise, you should always do the right thing. I know that having *friends and being around others is a good feeling.* 🗝 ² *People who uplift and encourage you to always do right are a blessing to have in your life. However, there are negative influences that can deter you from following my word and rules set for you. Keeping bad company will corrupt your good character.* 🗝 ³ *In other words, if you choose to hang around with bad people, they will lead you do things that you know are wrong and go against your morals. Do not allow others to tempt you. Temptation is wanting or doing something you know is wrong. You should not have to act out of character for acceptance by others. Choose your friends wisely and be aware of anyone who does not respect your boundaries because they could have ulterior motives. Sending and receiving inappropriate messages is not only dangerous but it goes against the guidelines your mom set for you. One of my commandments is to honor your father and mother. Obedience is a way to honor them. What do you think could have happened if Abram did not obey my order to relocate to a new town? Thankfully, he did not have to find out the answer to this question. Obedience will help you avoid harsh consequences and blessings can result. If it goes against my word or set rules, then you should avoid the person or act. In this way, you maintain your good character and are obedient. You will be content with your friendships, honor your mother, and maintain your mom's trust. I am pleased when you follow my word and obey your parents.*

Love, Your Heavenly Father

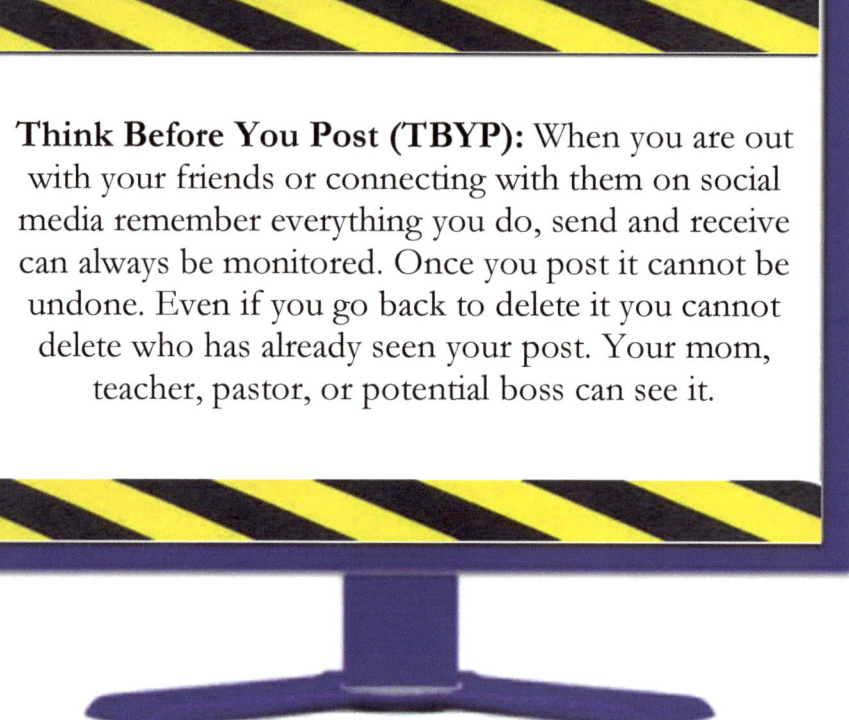

Think Before You Post (TBYP): When you are out with your friends or connecting with them on social media remember everything you do, send and receive can always be monitored. Once you post it cannot be undone. Even if you go back to delete it you cannot delete who has already seen your post. Your mom, teacher, pastor, or potential boss can see it.

Consider this before posting:
*Is it disrespectful? *Is it harmful?
*Is it appropriate? *Would my mom approve?

POWER OF THE TONGUE

Do not let any unwholesome talk come out of your mouths, but only what is helpful for building others up according to their needs, that it may benefit those who listen.
—Ephesians 4:29 NIV

Re: "Yes! Saturday morning. I can lay in my bed and watch television or ride my bike all day. No school, no chores." Arianna chanted as she adjusted her pillow under her head. Then she heard her mom say, "Good morning, Arianna" as she peaked in her room. You know you have not cleaned up your room all week. "You cannot watch television or go outside until it is cleaned," her mom said Arianna slowly got out of bed and stomped around her room. Then she yelled, "I never get to do what I want to do." She slammed the door. "I wish my dad was here." Her mom heard her but was too heartbroken to immediately respond.

Dear Daughter,

In the Bible, I asked Noah to build an ark to keep his family and the animals safe from a flood that I would send. Noah did not question my order and he did just as I instructed, carefully constructing the boat to my specifications. When the flood covered the earth, everyone and every animal except those on the ark were wiped away. If Noah had disobeyed my order he, his family and the animals would not have survived to repopulate the earth. In life, you will have to do some things that you do not want to do. In school, you may have homework on weekends. When you get a job, you may have to work when you don't feel like it. It is all a part of life. Chores are a way to help your mom out. Your attitude in response to doing something you don't want to do can either help or hurt the situation. Words are powerful. They can bring life to a situation or can kill a positive conversation. This is the reason everything you say should be kind and well thought out and chosen wisely. ᵎ Remember, it's difficult to put toothpaste back in the tube once its squeezed out. When you speak mean things to people you cannot take them back. You can apologize but the sting of your words still hurt. This is another reason forgiveness is necessary.

Love,

Your Heavenly Father

Proverbs 18:21

What you say can preserve life or destroy it; so, you must accept the consequences of your words.

Talk It Out

When you say something that hurts someone you should apologize. Go hug you mom and apologize for hurting her feelings.

Fill It Out

Complete the Crossword Puzzle on the next page.

LIFE

Crossword puzzle clues

Down:

1. _____ make it easier

2. Accountable

3. _____ is unconditional

6. Small jobs at home

7. In place

9. Female child

Across:

4. Mental state

5. Learning institution

8. Ability

10. Appreciation

11. Not dependent on others

Daddy, do you love me?

HOW COULD YOU LEAVE ME?

Then God's peace, which goes beyond anything we can imagine, will guard your thoughts and emotions through Christ Jesus.
—Philippians 4:7 GW

R: Arianna was having a good day. Music blasted as she relaxed in her room. Arianna replaced the word *mom* in the lyrics with *dad* as she sang along. This song sums up how I feel about my *dad*, she thought.

"I don't get it. I know you are gone, but I can still feel you. I got a picture in my room and it kills me, but I don't need a picture of my [dad] I need the real thing." -NF

Dear Daughter,

Your life is not make-believe, and the reality of how things are can be very difficult. People will come and go in your life. Their choice may be voluntary or involuntary, you do not have control over this. Regardless of who enters or leaves your life, no matter the situation, you can always trust me to be there with you. I will provide you peace when you focus on me and not on problems you face. One day, Jesus and his disciples took a boat out to sea. While Jesus slept, a storm came. Water covered the boat, and the disciples were afraid. They woke Jesus up and said, "Lord, save us." Jesus rebuked the storm and said, "Peace be still." [1] The wind and the waters became calm, and they all were saved.

Peace is what I give to you when you are going through a storm, feeling frustrated, emotional, or have questions that you cannot get answers to. Don't let the absence of your dad stir up worry or stress. Instead, talk to me and trust in me to give you peace just as Jesus did to his disciples in the face of a storm. Focus on my promises and the blessings I have given to you. Rejoice in the fact that I love you, and you are my child. Take comfort in knowing that I will take care of you all the days of your life. Doesn't it feel good to know that I will never leave you or allow storms to overtake you?

Love,
Your Heavenly Father

Pictures are visual ways to remember times you shared with others.

Think about the music that you like to listen to? Is it disrespectful. or degrading? You should choose to listen to music that uplifts and pushes you to be the best despite any situation. On the lines below, write the titles of songs that motivate and encourage you especially when you are feeling down. On a separate sheet of paper write out the lyrics to the songs. Use this list when you need it to be encouraged.

1. _____
2. _____
3. _____
4. _____
5. _____

Write it out. Writing allows you to express how you are feeling, describe the moment you are in and release emotions that clear your mind. Writing is healing.

BE BOLD

When I called, you answered me. You made me bold by strengthening my soul.
—Psalm 138:3 GW

R: Arianna was so proud of her accomplishments. She made it through her high school freshman year. Straight A's, a member of the marching band, basketball team, and track. She was equally happy for her mom who published her first book. Arianna's mom asked her to share how the book has impacted her life. Arianna visualized herself speaking in front of her peers and she was nervous about agreeing to do it. "Mom, adults will be in the audience too. Don't you think I am too young to talk to them? What if I mess up my words or no one listens to me? Mom, do you really think I will be able to talk in front of my friends? I don't think I can do it. I know your book is based on the reality of my life, and I know how to deal with questions about my dad much better than when I was in middle school, but I don't know mom," she said.

Daddy, do you love me?

Dear Daughter,

Speaking at your mom's book signing is a great way to show my love in action. You have been through some difficult times as you lived with the absence of your dad, and you have overcome feelings of abandonment. You are not too young to share your story and my word. [1] *I have equipped and qualified you to speak to your peers and others about this.* [2] *I have given you everything you need to share your story of strength and resilience. This is a great opportunity to tell your testimony and encourage other girls just as your mom and I have encouraged you. I promised to always be with you, and I will not break my promise. Stand firm in faith, be courageous and know that you can do all things through me, your heavenly Father who strengthens you.* [3]

Love,
Your Heavenly Father

Joshua 1:9 NLT

This is my command -- be strong and courageous! Do not be afraid or discouraged. For the LORD your God is with you wherever you go.

WRITE IT OUT

Write a journal entry about what you will share with other girls your age who miss their dad and wonder if he loves them.

JOURNAL ENTRY

Today's Date _____

_____
_____
_____
_____
_____
_____
_____
_____
_____
_____

Daddy, do you love me?

LETTERS OF LOVE

I'm not writing this to make you feel ashamed but to instruct you as my dear children.
—1 Corinthians 4:14 GW

Re: Ninth grade graduation day came. Arianna was proud of the great job she did all year. Arianna shared with her mom the excitement she felt. She was happy that her grandparents, aunts and uncles were traveling to celebrate with her. "I wish my dad could see me now," Arianna said softly.

Arianna's mom smiled and said, "I am proud of you. Despite all odds, I knew you could do it." "You know mom, before I faced the reality of my dads' absence, I felt all alone. Now, I feel empowered and confident that God has the best plan for my life. If I follow God and am grateful for all the blessings He has given me and only focus on what I can control, then the absence of my father will not have a negative impact on my life. I may never understand the reason my *dad*

left me. But, I do know for sure that God is love, God loves me, and He has all power over anything and any situation that seeks to destroy me or keep me out of His will. If He sees fit that my dad will be a positive part of my life, then He will reunite us. Yes, Mom, this is what I want to tell other girls." Arianna said. You know what, mom," Arianna said. "I will write an open letter for girls' whose reality is like mine. I pray these girls will also know they are wanted and loved. No matter what, I want other girls to know they should never give up, never settle, aim high and always share God's love wherever they go. I will also write to dads who choose not to be a part of their daughters' lives. I hope my letters will encourage absent dads to reach out to their daughters. God placed them on this earth with a special purpose in mind."

Dear Girls,

"The reality is that my life isn't perfect. Even before he left, I never had a full-time dad. That was hard for me. So, when he just disappeared and left me, I completely broke down. I thought, why doesn't he love me and how could he leave his seven year

old daughter? Thinking about him always brought me to a dark place. But through all this hatred and self-doubt, I realized that the one person who has always been there was my mom. Yes, it was still hard for me, but I could always just go to her with things. She did extra to fill in the gap. People underestimate single moms. They don't have a track record of their successes. So now the reality is if I ever think of my dad, instead of emptiness, I feel warmth knowing my mommy, will always be there."
(Lovingly submitted by Armanni Welch)
Love in Action,
Arianna

Dear Absent Dads,

    First, to my dad Mr. Yorn: I am older now and I know what a deadbeat parent means. No, my mother is not scorned. She has never said a negative word about you in my presence. I have formed my own opinion of you. A deadbeat parent is one who neglects his child. He is irresponsible and has no concern for his child. He is aware that his child misses him and yearns for quality time with him, but it does not matter to him. The fact of your absence qualifies you as a deadbeat. You abandoned me. You neglected me. You never call, write, or visit.

I know you are out there somewhere, and I know you remember my presence. Do you recall the day you abandoned me? I remember it so clearly. Here's my last memory of the day you never showed to pick me up from school. It was the worst day of my life. I waited and waited. You never called, never came by my mother's house. When my mom called you repeatedly you didn't even answer the phone. Didn't I deserve an explanation? How could you leave me? Almost eight years later and still nothing from you. I thank God for the ability to forgive. There is so much power in letting go and not holding grudges. I'm empowered today because I have learned that God provides whenever I lack. I am thankful for a loving and caring mom, family and friends who continue to take care of me.

Secondly, to absent dads: Is your daughter still wondering why you left her? Doesn't she deserve an explanation? Do you even care? Do you love her? Just like me, your daughter misses you. Certain times of the year are more difficult than others to deal with. For me, every birthday I celebrate and every holiday especially Father's Day, is a repeat of the year before. I secretly wait for him to reach out to me only to be disappointed. I cannot reach out to him because he vanished. Every award ceremony, every game, I look in the audience to see his face. Only to be let down because he is never there. Absent dad, I don't know how you live each day without knowing the status of your daughter's life, but we will continue to grow and be strong. God has taught us that He is love and with Him we will never lack. With God leading us and other family members helping to take care of us, and handling what we have control over, we will be all that we are destined to be. The actions other people take toward us shows us love. Promises from God have comforted us and keeps us from hating you. Our prayer is that you will seek God with all your heart and pray for forgiveness. I pray that you replace any hate with love and compassion. If it is in God's will and we shall reconnect, we hope that that you seize the opportunity. However, if this does not occur, we will rest knowing that we, your daughters, are not the reason for your disappearance. We are still blessed and grateful for the earthly father figures present in our lives. We are thankful that God provides and fills any voids. As older daughters who are living without your daily presence and constant support we know what it means to have a deadbeat parent. We know how it feels to be abandoned, ridiculed, hurt, questioned about your existence, musically reminded of your absence and fatherless. Even in these feelings you should know, Daddy, we love you.

On behalf of daughters everywhere,

Arianna

Dear Daughter,

I know your situation and I am making provision for you. I have shown you my love by surrounding you with a mom who will do everything she can for you and other family, friends, teachers, and mentors that will support you. ¹ Continue to read and meditate on my word. ² Allow my scriptures teach you my ways and correct your wrongs. ³ These scriptures I leave are my promises to you so that you will be confident and know that you can do all things because I have empowered you. I see that you are sharing my love with the letters you wrote to girls and dads who have abandoned their daughters. This is a great step in self-healing and for helping others learn to heal. Applying my word to your reality will defeat Satan's tactics every time. You are my child and I love you.

Love,
Your Heavenly Father

Unconditional love is loving someone even when they hurt you, leave you, or don't do what is expected of them. God commands us to love each other regardless of our emotions or feelings.

Love Notes

Daddy, do you love me?

WRITE IT OUT
Write an open letter to absent dads.

Dear Absent Dads,

On behalf of daughters everywhere,
(Sign your name)

THE POINT OF IT ALL

Keep in mind that the Lord your God is [the only] God. He is a faithful God, who keeps his promise and is merciful to thousands of generations of those who love him and obey his commands.
—Deuteronomy 7:9 GW

From Arianna's Mom

My dear sweet girl,

You are precious and a joy to be with. I love being your mom, and I would not change it for anything. I am proud of you and I smile happy whenever I think of the young lady that you are becoming. Daughter, it is important to address your feelings about your dad. Some girls who grow up without a healthy relationship with their dads make unhealthy relationship choices, have a fear of abandonment, isolation, confusion, and have trust issues as adults. You see simply ignoring a problem does not make it go away. Acknowledge and take action against these possible negative outcomes. Arianna experienced signs of these issues, but she allowed the word of God to direct her in a positive direction. She applied scripture and was then able to overcome in several areas. She could face the question of where her dad was. She made new friends and encouraged them. She celebrated and enjoyed those who included her in their life. Most of all, she forgave her dad and moved on.

You too can be resilient and beat any challenges you face. You begin to heal when you talk about any issues you have with a trusted adult. Do not settle for less than God's best for your life. When you meet other girls, who have been abandoned by a parent, share God's word with them. Whenever you need to talk to God, just whisper a prayer. He is listening and is always *ready to hear from you. Trust in God with all your heart and do not depend on your own understanding. Acknowledge God, and He will direct your paths.* 🔎¹ *Even when people let you down, have faith and know that God will take care of you. Take life one day at a time. Don't rush living, and don't become impatient. God knows the plans He has for you, and they are to give you a hope and a future. The birds in the trees don't worry about where their food will come from, and the flowers don't worry about getting water to grow. Don't you know that God cares about you just as He cares for and supplies the needs of birds and flowers?* 🔎² *Never doubt His word, rather meditate on it. The Bible contains God's purpose, answers, promises, and instructions for living on His earth. It is His letter of love to you. God will fulfill His word. Celebrate your wins and ask for forgiveness when you mess up. Don't* use excuses or place blame. Don't focus on who left you. Be comforted in knowing God will never leave you alone. Be bold in your faith. Think positive thoughts even when the way looks bleak. Use the power of your tongue to speak life to dead situations. Do not limit yourself with statistics of being raised in a single-parent home without your dad. You have just as much potential as anyone who comes from a two-parent home. God loves you and He placed the right people in your life at the right time to show you that you are a beautiful girl who is loved and wanted. Do not accept anyone's opinion that goes against the word of God. You are chosen, and you're fearfully and wonderfully made. You are cherished and the apple of God's eye. Carry His light in your smile. You can overcome any obstacle when you stay focused and believe in the promises God has made to you. Your heavenly Father loves you and your mom and other family members do too.

Love,

Arianna's Mom

Dear Daughter,

Think on these things: You are not inferior. You are not at a disadvantage because your dad is absent from your life. You are my child and entitled to the promises that I have declared in my word. You must have faith and put in the work for your dreams to come true. Keep me first in everything you do. Continue to honor your dad despite his absence from your life. Share my love through kindness, gentleness and humbleness. Follow my commandments and you will continue to experience my blessings. ℘ ³ No matter, what you are my child. And the point of it all is I love you.

Love,

Your Heavenly Father

Read It Out

Use the verses on the next two pages to encourage yourself when you have emotions that you need help dealing with.

WHEN YOU FEEL . . . THE BIBLE SAYS

If you pray do not worry. If you worry do not pray. Replace doubt  with the word of God. You are destined for greatness.

-Arianna

WHEN YOU FEEL...	THE BIBLE SAYS...
Abandoned	Be strong and courageous. Don't tremble! Don't be afraid of them! The LORD your God is the one who is going with you. He won't abandon you or leave you. **Deuteronomy 31:6 GW**
Attacked	What, then, shall we say in response to these things? If God is for us, who can be against us? **Romans 8:31 NIV**
Confused	For God is not the author of confusion, but of peace. **1 Corinthians 14:33 KJV**
Disappointed	For I know the plans I have for you, declares the LORD, plans to prosper you and not to harm you, plans to give you hope and a future. **Jeremiah 29:11**
Doubt	If you need wisdom, ask our generous God, and he will give it to you. He will not rebuke you for asking. **James 1:5 NLT**

WHEN YOU FEEL...	THE BIBLE SAYS...
Fatherless	A father to the fatherless, a defender of widows, is God in his holy dwelling. **Psalm 68:5 NIV**
Fear	Don't be afraid, because I am with you. Don't be intimidated; I am your God. I will strengthen you. I will help you. I will support you with my victorious right hand. **Isaiah 41:10 GW**
Hate	My command is this: Love each other as I have loved you. **John 15:12 NIV**
Hurt	I am hurt and lonely. Turn to me and show me mercy. Free me from my troubles. Help me solve my problems. **Psalm 25:16-17 ERV**
Lost	Lord, help me learn your ways. Show me how you want me to live. Guide me and teach me your truths. You are my God, my Savior. **Psalm 25:4-5 ERV**
Not Good Enough	The LORD your God is with you. He is a hero who saves you. He happily rejoices over you, renews you with his love, and celebrates over you with shouts of joy. **Zephaniah 3:17 GW**
Overwhelmed	Commit everything you do to the LORD. Trust him, and he will help you. **Psalm 37:5**
Powerless	God, who shows you his kindness and who has called you through Christ Jesus to his eternal glory, will restore you, strengthen you, make you strong, and support you as you suffer for a little while. **1 Peter 5:10**

WHEN YOU FEEL...	THE BIBLE SAYS...
Tempted	There isn't any temptation that you have experienced which is unusual for humans. God, who faithfully keeps his promises, will not allow you to be tempted beyond your power to resist. But when you are tempted, he will also give you the ability to endure the temptation as your way of escape. **1 Corinthians 10:13 GW**
Unforgiveable	Make allowance for each other's faults and forgive anyone who offends you. Remember, the Lord forgave you, so you must forgive others. **Colossians 3:13 NLT**
Weak	This is my command--be strong and courageous! Do not be afraid or discouraged. For the LORD your God is with you wherever you go. **Joshua 1:9 NLT**
Worried	Give all your worries and cares to God, for he cares about you. **1 Peter 5:7 NLT**

Finally, daughter see yourself as God sees you. The handle on the mirror describes false things about you. Read the message in the mirror and use it as a reminder each day. "When you feel inferior. The Word of God says you are better than that.
-Arianna's Mom

Daddy, do you love me?

WHEN YOU WONDER DADDY, DO YOU LOVE ME? REMEMBER. . .

 You are God's own creation and you are loved by many.

You are human, not perfect. You may make mistakes.

You are worthy of respect. You are wonderfully made.

Things may not go as planned. People you love may

go away.

People you like may not feel the same way.

Living is easier when you forgive and let go.

Love without limits.

Learn from your mistakes. Accept wise counsel.

When the way looks dim. Seek God for direction.

Rest well.

Wake up to fight another day. Make your mark.

Have a positive impact on the world.

You are loved.

Unconditionally.

Anita Renee Murray

                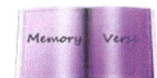

REFLECT ON GOD'S WORD
BIBLE SCRIPTURE REFERENCE

(In order of appearance in book)

The Wait

All praise to God, the Father of our Lord Jesus Christ. God is our merciful Father and the source of all comfort. —2 Corinthians 1:3

Whisper A Prayer

Then you will call on me and come and pray to me, and I will listen to you. You will seek me and find me when you seek me with all your heart.[1] —Jeremiah 29:12 NIV

Therefore, I tell you, whatever you ask for in prayer, believe that you have received it, and it will be yours.[2] —Mark 11:24 NIV

Day By Day

Have I not commanded you? Be strong and courageous. Do not be afraid; do not be discouraged, for the LORD your God will be with you wherever you go. —Joshua 1:9

Rude Girls

I have many aggressive enemies; they hate me without reason.[1]

—Psalm 38:19 NLT

The second most important commandment is this: Love your neighbor as you love yourself. No other commandment is greater than these.[2]

—Mark 12:31 GW

A gentle answer turns away rage, but a harsh word stirs up anger.[3]

—Proverbs 15:1 GW

Remember this, my dear brothers and sisters: Everyone should be quick to listen, slow to speak, and should not get angry easily. An angry person doesn't do what God approves of. [4]   —James 1:19-20 GW

What Color Is Your Dress?

The LORD is my strength and my shield; my heart trusts in him, and he helps me. My heart leaps for joy, and with my song I praise him.

—Psalm 28:7 NIV

June

Father to the fatherless, defender of widows--this is God, whose dwelling is holy.   —Psalm 68:5 NLT

Excuses

You watch me when I travel and when I rest. You are familiar with all my ways.[1]   —Psalm 139:3 GW

Your eyes saw me when I was still an unborn child. Every day of my life was recorded in your book before one of them had taken place.[2]

—Psalm 139:16 GW

Finally, brothers, whatever is true, whatever is honorable, whatever is just, whatever is pure, whatever is lovely, whatever is commendable, if there is any excellence, if there is anything worthy of praise, think about these things.[3]   —Philippians 4:8

And we know- that for those who love God all things work together for good, for those who are called according to his purpose.[4]

—Romans 8:28

And those he predestined, he also called; those he called, he also justified; those he justified, he also glorified.[5]

—Romans 8:30 NIV

Celebrate

Take my yoke upon you. Let me teach you, because I am humble and gentle at heart, and you will find rest for your souls[1]

—Matthew 11:29 NLT

Let all bitterness and wrath and anger and clamor and slander be put away from you, along with all malice. Be kind to one another, tenderhearted, forgiving one another, as God in Christ forgave you.[2]

—Ephesians 4:31-32 ESV

The Question

O Lord, you have examined my heart and know everything about me. You know when I sit down or stand up. You know my thoughts even when I'm far away. You see me when I travel and when I rest at home. You know everything I do.[1]

—Psalm 139:1-3 NLT

You keep track of all my sorrows. You have collected all my tears in your bottle. You have recorded each one in your book.[2]

—Psalm 56:8

IChat

Beware of false prophets who come disguised as harmless sheep but are really vicious wolves.[1]

—Matthew 7:15 NLT

My thoughts are nothing like your thoughts," says the LORD.
And my ways are far beyond anything you could imagine.[2]

—Isaiah 55:8 NLT

You Are Not Alone

So God created human beings in his own image. In the image of God he created them; male and female he created them.[1]

—Genesis 1:27 NLT

Even every hair on your head has been counted. Don't be afraid! You are worth more than many sparrows.[2]   —Luke 12:7

And my God will supply every need of yours according to his riches in glory in Christ Jesus.[3]   --Philippians 4:19 ESV

Messed Up

I'll make you a great nation and bless you. I'll make you famous; you'll be a blessing.[1]   —Genesis 12:2 MSG

Two are better than one, because they have good pay for their work. For if one of them falls, the other can help him up. But it is hard for the one who falls when there is no one to lift him up.[2]

—Ecclesiastes 4:9-10 NLT

Abram passed through the country as far as Shechem and the Oak of Moreh. At that time the Canaanites occupied the land. Do not be misled: "Bad company corrupts good character.[3]

1 Corinthians 15:33 NIV

Power of the Tongue

Everything you say should be kind and well thought out so that you know how to answer everyone.

—Colossians 5:6

How Could You Leave Me?

And he awoke and rebuked the wind and said to the sea, "Peace! Be still!" And the wind ceased, and there was a great calm.

—Mark 4:39

Letters of Love

Give me a sign of your goodness, that my enemies may see it and be put to shame, for you, LORD, have helped me and comforted me.[1]

—Psalm 86: 17

Keep this Book of the Law always on your lips; meditate on it day and night, so that you may be careful to do everything written in it. Then you will be prosperous and successful.[2]

—Joshua 1:8

Every Scripture passage is inspired by God. All of them are useful for teaching, pointing out errors, correcting people, and training them for a life that has God's approval.[3]

—2 Timothy 3:16

Be Bold

The Lord replied, "Don't say, 'I'm too young,' for you must go wherever I send you and say whatever I tell you.[1]

—Jeremiah 1:7 NLT

Equip you with everything good for doing his will, and may he work in us what is pleasing to him, through Jesus Christ, to whom be glory for ever and ever. Amen.[2]

—Hebrews 13:21

For I can do everything through Christ, who gives me strength.³

—Philippians 4:13

The Point of It All

In all your ways acknowledge Him, And He shall direct your paths.¹

-Proverbs 3:6 NJKV

Look at the birds in the sky. They do not plant seeds. They do not gather grain. They do not put grain into a building to keep. Yet your Father in heaven feeds them! Are you not more important than the birds? Which of you can make himself a little taller by worrying? Why should you worry about clothes? Think how the flowers grow. They do not work or make cloth.²

—Matthew 6:26-28

You can make this choice by loving the Lord your God, obeying him, and committing yourself firmly to him. This is the key to your life. And if you love and obey the Lord, you will live long in the land the LORD swore to give your ancestors Abraham, Isaac, and Jacob.³

—Deuteronomy 30:20 NLT

ABOUT THE AUTHOR

Anita Renee Murray is an author and inspirationalist. She writes to edify girls to prevent negativity, jealously, hate and low self-esteem, to empower women to never settle for less than God's best for them and encourage females to have confidence in themselves and to reach their full potential. With a passion for speaking to teens and young adults about abstinence and healthy relationships, Renee is the founder of Teens Before Parents, a recommended speaker, certified facilitator and mentor. Renee lives in Spartanburg, SC with her husband Wayne, and their daughter Armanni.

www.ingramcontent.com/pod-product-compliance
Lightning Source LLC
Chambersburg PA
CBHW042336150426
43195CB00001B/12